STRONG WINDS AT MISHI PASS

STRONG WINDS
AT MISHI PASS

Poems by
Tong-Gyu Hwang

Translated by
Seong-Kon Kim & Dennis Maloney

White Pine Press · Buffalo, New York

WHITE PINE PRESS
P.O. Box 236, Buffalo, New York 14201

First Edition

Publication of this book was made possible, in part,
with public funds from the
New York State Council on the Arts, a State Agency,
and with the generous support of
The Daesan Foundation.

Book design: Elaine LaMattina

Printed and bound in the United States of America

Library of Congress Control Number:
2001091832

INTRODUCTION
Tong-Gyu Hwang:
Traveling Poet Who Defeats Death - 7

I. STRONG WINDS AT MISHI PASS (1993)

II: from *Journey to Morundae* (1991)

III: Wind Burial Poems & Love Poems (1991-1993)

TONG-GYU HWANG:
TRAVELING POET WHO DEFEATS DEATH

Few Korean readers would deny that Tong-Gyu Hwang is one of the most prominent and influential Korean poets alive today. Since his literary debut in 1958, Hwang has always occupied a central place in the history of Korean poetry. He has published ten very important collections of work and won numerous prestigious awards, including the famous Modern Literature Award, the Korean Literature Award, the Isan Literature Award, and the Daesan Literary Award.

A literary critic once called Hwang "a poet of rebellion and change." This is, in some ways, very true. Hwang is a poet who constantly rebels against tradition while seeking innovation. Indeed, one of the most interesting aspects of Hwang and his work is the way his revolt and search for something new and different seem to continuously perpetuate themselves. Thus, an innovation which originated from Hwang's rebellion is deconstructed by another of his rebellions. This then leads to another innovation that will, again, be dismantled and destroyed. "I don't want to mold my life or my poetry," says Hwang, "for they exist as constantly progressing forms."

Tong-Gyu Hwang's works, however, are too multifaceted for him to be categorized solely as a poet of rebellion and change. It is then, perhaps, more befitting to describe him as a poet on a journey, someone who is constantly on the move. Delineation of Hwang as a poet on a journey seems particularly apt due to the journey as one of his recurrent themes. In fact, the recurrence of the journey motif is so frequent that readers may associate themselves as fellow travelers on the poet's spiritual journey. This spiritual journey transcends all existing boundaries and eventually goes to the heart of not only nature but also of human nature. For the poet, therefore, traveling is like writing a poem and is also a symbolic act of revolting against a fixed reality, seeking freedom and change, exploring his own identities and finally encountering his inner self.

The celebrated Wind Burial poems are perfect examples of this. The Wind Burial poems took Hwang fourteen years to complete. These serial poems are a travel log of the poet's spiritual journey to the unknown realm of life and death. Through this work, the poet confronts, transcends, and finally embraces death, reaching the truly heightened level of Nirvana. The Wind Burial poems, with their affirmation and overcoming of death, enable the reader to obtain sheer spiritual freedom, that is, freedom from the fear of death and the contradictions of life.

Hwang's spiritual journey takes place not only in pastoral backgrounds but also in his mundane everyday life. Thus, the Hwang's poetry is irrevocably tied to the thing it seeks to escape: the city. It is where the poet suddenly finds the exquisite moonlight and the warm human touch. Though the poet may be physically in his car, his office or even at his home, spiritually he is "on the road," searching for the pastoral even in the city's asphalt jungle. What he finds at the end of his journey, however, is a strong wind that embraces both the city and the pastoral, the secular and the pure, and ultimately, life and death.

The poet's journey may be a revolt against reality but it is by no means an escape from it. This can be evidenced by the fact that although he always drives his car to the "heart of nature," he eventually returns to the city where he belongs. By placing his car, a machine, next to "heart of nature" he strongly evokes the image of the "machine in the garden." The poet's car, then, may be a necessary evil that one detests but cannot do without, just like the locomotive that disturbs Thoreau's meditation in Walden.

Hwang's poetry depicts the transcendence of all arbitrary boundaries between seemingly contradictory oppositions, such as life and death, nature and civilization, and the mundane and the celestial. It is precisely this dual vision of the poet that ultimately brings forth a whole new world of reconciliation to a reality full of conflict and contradiction. Such remarkable poetic capacity and intricacy make Tong-Gyu Hwang a truly appealing poet to Asian and Western readers alike.

—Seong-Kon Kim and Dennis Maloney
Buffalo, New York
July 1, 2001

PART I:
STRONG WINDS AT MISHI PASS
(1993)

Dream Flower

Shepherd's purse and sandwort,
The smallest flowers I have ever seen,
Bloom side by side,
Whispering, "I'm poorer than you."
Look closely. They smile serenely.
Not a single petal-tooth fallen,
Every face is beautiful.

One weekend afternoon, all my colleagues gone,
As I nodded off to sleep on the hill near my office,
Someone asked,
Who are you? What flower?
"A dream flower,"
I answered sleepily.
A dream flower so small
You see it only when you're lonely,
(My teeth fall out quietly.)
Though it always blooms near you.

Meeting Wonhyo at O-Uh Temple

1

If you plan to visit O-uh Temple
You should spend some idle time in P'ohang first.
How could you go directly to the temple,
Where Wonhyo enjoyed serenity, fishing with his friends?
Act foolishly. First visit the rusty sea,
Eat seafood stew,
Watch cargo ships unload.
At a cheap alley tavern near the seafood restaurant
Break dried sardines into tiny pieces,
Dip them in hot sauce, and eat.
Finally, down a glass of *soju*.
Ah, you should roam the city first,
Finding that restaurant without knowing its address.
Every time you circle around
And ask for its location,
You'll be told something else.
When you're on the verge of giving up,
You'll meet a taxi driver who knows the way.
The alleys near the station are as wandering and complex
As the life of Wonhyo himself,
Who shaved his hair then grew it back again,
Then after that left it alone.

2

Is there anyone who's not essentially a wanderer?
What makes us wide awake at two a.m.?
Why do we struggle with the typewriter all night long?
Why stay up until dawn? To water the orchid late at night?

3
Fifteen miles from P'ohang
The road is as smooth
As the sky.
My car runs so quietly the bottom of my mind peels away,
But before my brain begins to rattle,
Mt. Unje appears on my right.
I drive around the lake
And approach the temple of O-Uh.

4
Wait!
I see the wondrous reflection of Mt. Unje
Upside down in the lake.
Ah, reflection of the temple itself!
Someone whispers in my ear:
"You should see everything upside down once,
It gives you a different perspective.
Is it O-uh temple or Uh-o?
Is it a temple at all?"
I glance up. Another steep cliff.

5
In a corner of the main temple I see
A relic: a Buddhist monk's hat made of fine grass.
Fourteen hundred years ago.
It's Wonhyo's hat.
I see his old spoon, dark with verdigris.
Again I visit the lake. Several carp
That Wonhyo and his friends would have caught and eaten raw
Swim in the dead-calm lake.
One fish raises its head at my feet.
Such dignity!
The temple becomes Wonhyo's name.
Because Wonhyo is not here.

Like a Thief, I Drove My Jeep at Night

Like a thief, I drove my Jeep at night
Toward Wonhyo Hermitage
The headlights conspired with the wet brush
That constantly beat against the fenders of the Jeep.
The steep and narrow road looked like a cul de sac at every turn,
Just a dim space neither clearly visible nor totally unseen.
The crescent moon, in clouds, hid then peeked.
My Jeep bumped over the last rocky stretch.
I took a deep breath, turned off the engine and the lights.
In the moonlight, O-Uh Temple and the lake
had fallen deeply asleep
Holding each other tight.
Shall I steal them silently
And put them in my Jeep?

The sound of birds in their troubled sleep.

The House of Ho Nansolhon

Standing near the house where Ho Nansolhon was born,
in Chodang-dong, Kangnung,
I see a trumpet flower with withered leaves.

The paper of the sliding door is torn
The entire house is empty,
And so is time.
The butterflies and bees are gone.
Her friends,
And her brother Gyun's friends are long gone, too.
Only a rickety ladder used for apple picking remains,
Leaning on one leg against a tree.
Just one small juniper
Crouching in the yard crawls endlessly

The Last Poem

On the obsidian tombstone
A scrawling line stops short,
Never reaching the edge.
Hesitating a moment
Where bits of blue quartz shine,
The line changes direction
Then crawls a few inches more.

Someday, I'll leave my crawling poem..

The Day We Buried Kim Hyon

—Remember that day?

Returning from the funeral of Kim Hyon,
Even monsoon clouds briefly vanished from the sky.
We sped at seventy through a forty-mile zone
As if hurrying away from our memories.
Remember the traffic cop who stopped us?
He was too young to read our complex minds.
We were hurrying away from the peacefully smiling face
Of Kim Hyon, so vivid and beautiful still,
who'd taken license to die and became a ghost.
We ignored the mountains' panoramic fashion show
And got a speeding ticket that day,
to outrun his death.

At My Friend's Grave

A year after our separation,
The sky finally clears,
Despite thick monsoon clouds.

Above bright clouds
Covered with tiny white flowers,
You live without being seen!

Kim Hyon's Real Name

Since you left this world, you've become difficult to reach.
Tomorrow marks three years since we buried you.
Tonight, in your memory
I open a bottle I saved in a secret place
And have a drink alone,
Listen to the Alban Berg Quartet on CD.
In this world, we've lived through three more years.
In a cloud castle embroidered
with tiny white flowers and butterflies,
you've remained the same.
You're laughing silently up there.
Do you have the movie *So Pyon Jye* there, too?
Oh, dear Kwangnam!

In Autumn

In autumn, I'll take the early bus,
Like a man who arrives too soon, thanks to light traffic,
and takes the first bus that leaves instead of waiting
for his scheduled route.
Passing ironweed beckoning on both sides of the road,
Leaving parti-colored maple trees behind,
Perplexed by unfamiliar scenes,
Like a leaf or a blood cell
That gently falls
On a small, luminous fruit stand in a corner of the public square,
But drifts a moment in air, losing its balance in the wind
Before finally touching the fruit.
I'll live that way and leave this world,
Not remembering why I came.

That's how I'll depart.

The Sound of Rain, Late Autumn

It's not the sound of raindrops
Falling on flowers, leaves, human flesh.
It's not the sound of raindrops
Colliding or rolling on the ground.
It's just the sound of raindrops
Falling intermittently on earth and quietly fading away.
A sound so dark the pupils of my eyes can't help but widen.
I see the roots of trees.
Roots that can't intertwine
And are stuck in the ground all alone.
I see the tangled roots of my innumerable follies and misdeeds.
A turtledove flaps its wings and flies away.
Ah, the sound of raindrops penetrates my heart!

The sound of time running out!

An Early Winter Night

An early winter night.
Outside the window wind drifts into sleep and so do people.
Across the street the streetlight begins to fade.
Only my nightlight stands gazing at the street below.
Ah, the moon is out, dim as a dying fluorescent lamp.
If I fall asleep well and choose the right path in my dream,
Perhaps I'll see the big moon again,
The moon I met joyfully and parted from reluctantly
On the outer edge of Seoul a while ago.
Ah, that familiar face!
(Suyuri and Sadang-dong might be good places to see the moon.)
Will I see her again?
If that doesn't work,
Should I drive alone once more,
To the country on a summer night
To find the bright moon unexpectedly hanging on my windshield
And pretend to be surprised?
If I can't see her because of smog
Should I abandon all round things this winter
And seek instead dried pollack on Daekwan Pass,
Hollow and hanging from the drying stand?

Here comes another dried one, his eyes wide open!

I Felt Like Driving on Icy Roads

I felt like driving on icy roads.
Thus I abruptly left home
And spent the day traveling to the mountains, which wear
        proper winter clothes,
Finally arriving at Bopju Temple on Mt. Songni.
The hill damaged last rainy season was all that awaited me.
For the first time in my life
The twin lion stone lamp was not there.
Ah, the sensuous waists of the two stone lions that held the lamp!
I pretended not to notice,
Like in a dream.

Next morning
The inn's yard was filled:
Snow pearls.

On Local Roads

Both Orpheus and Yun Sondo played good music.
For me, music's found in traveling.
I like the shimmering vibration of my small car on local roads.
Predicting an opposite car's drifting over the center lane on a sharp curve,
Swerving in time and swearing for a bit,
My mind knows peace and serenity,
Like being immersed in Kayakeum melody.
As I pass an ancient zelkova tree,
Like Orpheus, I quickly look back.
A motorcycle magnifies before my eyes, then disappears.

Strong Winds at Mishi Pass

—That day, Mishi Pass was a great wind itself.

1

Oh wind!
Without a wrinkle to grasp on the surface of the earth,
Without a single tree or bush or grass on which to cling,
Without a phrase of the sacred Book with which to live,
I swayed on Mishi Pass.

The whole landscape swayed in the wind,
As if it were wind itself.
Mt. Sorak swayed,
My backbone swayed, too.
I struggled to keep from blowing away,
Holding myself in my arms.

2

Every time I try to live aloof and detached,
The wind sweeps me away,
Relentlessly,
Often driving me away from the world.
Only the scarred roadside trees
And the signboards of pubs are my friends.
(The pubs I visit often move to another place or close.)
The wind diminishes.

3

Now, wind blows only in my dreams.
No, only outside my dreams. It blows, then vanishes.
Secretly breaking the pub signs,
Breaking the roadside trees,
Demolishing the birthplace of my dreams,
The wind falls into dreamless sleep.

4
When I think of the wind,
I dream of a small bird,
A bird the wind has forgotten to embrace.
I dream a face that will fly away and instantly disappear
When I gaze at the sky to see it.

That face will never age.
Indeed?

5
Something's wrong with the desk I lived with for twenty-three years.
Examining it, I find rust everywhere,
Edges, handles, legs,
Every nook and corner of the drawers.
Ah, it's my life's rust,
Everything that doesn't vanish rusts.
I take out my handkerchief and wipe my face.

The delivery boys who brought the new desk are gone.
Leaving my office,
I slip past the old desk left out in the hall.
Holding the desk's edge with both hands, I hold my breath,
Barely keep my balance.
Suddenly I see trees outside the window at the far end of the hall.
They've stood there, unnoticed, all this time.

The trees are quiet.
I run my hands carefully over the face of the old desk.
My guts, joints, brains are full of rust.
The tarnish spreads.
The tarnish runs down all sides.
I caress the face of my old desk again
Suddenly the earth's face softens.
Strange!

The wind begins to blow again.
The trees begin again to sway.
So do the signboards and the roadside trees.
The trees in Kangwon roar in pleasure.
The wind blows stronger each time,
Finally leaving my imagination behind.
Ah, this earth.

Strong winds at Mishi Pass.

A Conversation at "Five-Color Valley"

> When the earth quietly pull my sleeve,
> I want to leave this world,
> Strolling at Five-Color Valley on Mt. Sorak
> on a spring evening.
> —A Poet Must Live in Poverty, III

"When the flowers in Five-Color Valley wither, where would you die?"
Handing a gourd of spring water to me, my friend asks
Through the murmuring sound of a stream
I hear a few unfamiliar birds chirping.
"I will go find Six-Color Valley, then."
"Where is this Six-Color Valley?"
"Where there are no colorful flowers."

Seven Variations on Li Po's Main Theme

Spending the Night With a Friend

To wash away my cares
I loosen my belt and continue to drink.
The warm night invites friendly conversation
And the bright moon won't let me fall asleep.
Drunk, I lie down on the empty mountain,
a blanket of heaven, a pillow of earth.

—Li Po

1

With wine and snacks
I climb Mt. Saja with friends.
It's already late fall and autumn leaves have fallen on the ridge.
But their color is still spectacular on the road to Nirvana Pavilion.
In front of the pavilion we share a paper cup of wine.
Thank God! The pouch doesn't leak the cold *jin*.

2

My destiny, if you exist,
Please forget me for a moment
As I drive between Isu Bridge and Chongshin Station in Seoul.
Forget my age and driver's license number,
Forget that I'm moving as if driving the scenic highway at South Sea beach,
Spotting an attractive woman,
And momentarily dreaming a sensual dream.

3

I take out the Cognac bottle I left on the bookshelf long ago
And carefully twist the cork.
On a late autumn night, in an matchbox-size apartment
A dry match, a dry match is ready to flame!
After allowing the wine to breathe,
I send it down to my warm belly.

4

Occasionally the spring water I drank calls to me.
The mountains that provide spring water call me.
There's a temple in every valley of Mt. Odae,
And every temple has a natural spring for thirsty souls.
Scooping water through broken ice to drink, I shiver.
Will the water warm me somehow when my body stiffens cold?

5

These days I get drunk easily.
Perhaps now I can live frugally near the Han River.
In the past I needed wine to fall asleep.
Now the wine needs me.
On short spring evenings, let the television fall asleep
And the days I spend on the couch with my eyes closed increase.

6

In Yongmoon temple in Yangpyung in Kyongki
Lives a ticklish red tree,
And in Yongmoon temple in Namhae in Kyongnam
Lives a three-barrel cannon with three empty throats.
In the village below that temple,
A stone pagoda emerges from the ground like a bamboo shoot.
Spiritual things live everywhere in this world.
At dawn at the fish market in Samchunpo
Even beautiful fish holding their breaths with a sidelong glance
Will attract your soul.

7

The moon shows her face over the clouds briefly and then hides.
What is sky to moon, this sky of sparsely scattered stars?
Someday will people on the moon be kept awake by earth's light?
Can future man remain human if he's often sleepless at night?
Let the waning moon move on
And let's have a glass of wine, proud as two enduring moons.

Leibniz, Who Enjoyed Death

Autumn in Germany, and in the humid tower of Hanover Palace
You enjoyed death,
Fasting for several months.
Today while perusing the genealogy of the England's Hanover Dynasty
For my English literature class,
I remember how you baffled me with infinitesimal calculus
Drawing Europe's map in my high school days.
But you,
You didn't leave a grave in this world,
You who went underground, wrapped in ragged straw like a thief.

If we erased all graves, big and small, in this world
Would the earth be clean?
(Ah! Like a Buddhist nun's naked head!)

Natural Spring at Sambong

1

The brook at Hongchon in Kangwon,
When were our souls this crystal-clear?
My car crosses the brook, breaks the icy mirror beneath.
Birds, frowning, are sitting in the trees.
Will the natural spring at Sambong wait for me
In the middle of the wooden stairway,
Her right hand on her forehead, left hand on her waist?
When the brook's broken ice becomes a mirror again,
Birds will fly at their leisure in the bright sky
And the moon will smile during the day.

2

If the world moves like a broken watch,
I'll live in Hongchon
Near a quiet mountain path on a branch of Kyepang Creek.
The wind whispers: "Despair is sometimes an escape."
If I change the entrance sign,
It won't be hard to spend a couple winters there:
Instead of "Natural Spring,"
My sign will read, "Bohemians' Retreat:
Rest place for the bodies and souls of exotic fish
Doomed to die if they can't cool their fever in cold water."

Cicada

The song of a cicada
Who endured more than ten years beneath earth
Waiting for a pair of wings to sprout.
The song of a cicada
So cool and refreshing to my itchy skin.

I, too, have crawled on earth more than fifty years,
Many times packing and carrying my stuff,
Looking for a place to rent.
I, too, have wriggled, cried, raised my head to scream.
I, too, have seen dark spring flowers and autumn's bright hills.
O, I've barely begun to understand the meaning of silence.
O, after more than fifty years, I'm just beginning to sing!

A Cricket

A cricket chirped nightly on my veranda near the potted ficus tree.
Yesterday, it chirped feebly from the storage shed.
What made it move to that place,
When the loneliness of autumn is ripening?
Did it crawl through the living room,
Or did it fly?
I imagine it slowly walking across the living room,
Crossing the open veranda doorsill sometime during the day.
It must have hesitated in front of the television set,
For that strange instrument sheds light each night
On living creatures and furniture in the house.
Jumping toward it,
It would have tried to feel the smooth screen with its sensitive antennae.
Ah, but its vision must have dimmed!
Losing control, it must have landed clumsily on the cushion,
And fallen asleep for a while.
Then slowly it must have walked into the kitchen
And licked a stain of spilled tea on the floor.
It must have nodded as it looked back,
Passed through the doorway
And into the storage shed,
The most secluded place in my house.

Today its chirp is gone.

Wearing Rock Moss

— to my friend, Taesu Yi

The flesh that's covered my bones for fifty-five years,
Is in good shape and works nicely today,
Thanks, perhaps, to all the wine I drank last night.
Luckily the sun is out. The snowstorm stopped today.
Visiting a valley in Chukjang, you lead
As we climb to the wooden pavilion covered with moss
That stands next to a rock, like in a painting.
We leisurely drink wine and eat dried fish,
Waiting for lost time that runs well ahead of me.

In the sky a few clouds drift, time's signal.
In my glass, the wine is amazingly clear.
Rock moss wind is everywhere.

When My Knees Begin to Ache

Perhaps my knee joint has begun to dry.
These days, my left knee aches.
So I gave up the concrete road
And went back to the earthen path.
Ah, cushion of earth!
Evening primroses were in full bloom,
One already withering, though.
I examined it everywhere
But it didn't show any pain.
Finally, I dismantled it.
Oh, no. The ovary was...

Perhaps my knee joint's begun to dry.
I empty my heavy mind on the earth.

Staying Up All Night, Writing

1.
Vacation as an excuse, I stay up all night, writing.
By morning, manuscripts are scattered everywhere.
At daybreak
I open the window.
Through the mist
I see the mountain covered with several days' snow.
A winter like last winter.
I move my tongue across the inside of my cheek.
Skin touches skin.
Oh, a night of the tongue that underwent tanning.
Skin touches skin.

2
Last night in my writing
I switched all the "I's" to "he's."
Then, a small bag on his shoulder
He got off the bus
At Bopheung Temple on Mt. Saja.
The mountain's ridge burned with bright autumn leaves,
Newly naked trees stood like exquisite lace.
Both side ridges were spectacular,
Even the back ridge!
Passing the pavilion under construction, he took a mountain trail
Covered with red, brown, and yellow fallen leaves.
He took the path that passes the old main temple on the right,
Quenched his thirst with spring water
And climbed to Nirvana Pavilion.
There a phallic shape emerged,
Like the one on Mt. Odae, though poorer.
Strolling around
He looked into the pavilion. No Buddha there.
Suddenly he disappeared with the briefcase

And all the words written overnight became an echo,
Echo.
I am an echo of his mind!

3
In that same space,
The painter Ch'ang Wukjin got off the long-distance bus
Without a briefcase.
He pulled a hair clipper out of his pocket
And clipped the lace on the ridge.
(Those Buddhist nuns' naked heads!)
Then he mixed the colors of autumn leaves,
Producing bright gray with which he drew a road,
Built a house with three lines as corner stones,
And drew a magpie in the empty sky above.
Beside the house stood a stick-figure man
Drawn with the line meant for the fourth corner stone.
Ah, it is "he."
Then he quietly became me.

4
My coffee tastes sweet.
So do my two aspirin.
I spit them into the sink.
Ah, am I addicted, after all, to scenic views?
Does it matter if the mountain's capped with last year's snow?
What if it's next year's?
Would it matter if the peak of Mt. Saja was barren in memory?
What if time's barren, too?
Or what if my words become his?
It isn't writing;
It's the touch of my tanned tongue against the inside of my cheek
That awakens me
To the sensations of life.
The whole house murmurs, waking up.

A Wandering Star

Although astronomers seem to value stars more than planets,
I value the fresh scent and warmth of planet earth.
Wandering around Kimpo and Kanghwa in late spring.
Iris bloomed like colored paintbrushes along the road.
At the foot of the hill, hydrangea bloomed abundantly,
Smiling over all.
They smiled even when I approached.
Climbing Mt. Mani in the middle of the night,
I saw an explosion of stars.
The dim scent of a wandering star clung to the slope.

On Earth

Spending the night in a rural village,
I'm unable to fall asleep. I open the window.
Birds chirp in the thick fog above the reservoir.
The sound is familiar but I've forgotten the name of the bird.
Is it owl or cuckoo?
Or a lonely singer
Lost in the fog?

Often I'm lost, too.
Sometimes, even in my own town.

I try so hard
But I can't remember the names and faces.
As I wander earth
We'll see one another again, for sure.
And though we might not remember a name,
We'll smile as we pass by.

The Devil

1

The devil whispers to my soul.
Don't look back.
Don't look back.
It's time. Go to your classroom with the roll book and text.

I approach the bookshelf but grab another book:
Fantastic Driving Courses.

The lips of all the flowers are wet with honey
A stream of honey runs off my tongue, too.
The flowers smelled so sweet
I secretly licked their insides.
the devil wouldn't know my secret likings..

2

The devil whispers:
Don't drink cheap liquor.
Don't touch Jinro, Bohae, Keumbokju, or Kyongwol.

Yesterday I drank faux Chivas Regal, though,
And became more drunk than usual.
Almost unconscious,
I took subway number three in the wrong direction
And arrived the terminal in the middle of the night.
Mt. Pukhan was veiled in the thick fog.
I wandered through the spring night as if lost in space.

3

An FM radio station broadcasts that it's raining,
But it's only overcast outside my study.

I turn the radio off and calm down.
But the devil isn't coming.

Has he forgotten my number?
I haven't heard from him for a while.
Right, I'll sneak away to the mountains
And play with the small but pretty
(My mouth waters)
Shepherd's purse and sandwort.

But before I can climb the mountain
Someone suddenly calls to me.
Ah! It's the devil!
Poof! I'm back in class.

Reading Your Memoir of My Younger Days

To My fellow traveler, Mah Chongki

Your memoir describes me as suave and special
When it swerves from reality.
So I won't think of you today,
I'll drive down local roads
Taking steep and unfamiliar paths
Which don't exist on any map.

Celebrated artist Ch'ang Wukjin, whom you respect, passed away.
For a moment, the whole world
Almost became Ch'ang Wukjin himself, but he didn't.
I frame a print of his painting, "A House and a Magpie"
To look at whenever life is dreary.
Summer has come.

At the edge of Mt. Odae I parked my car.
A pine-needle carpet spreads above the natural spring.
Like a spider flying above it,
I airily flew and flew.
Someone flew.

My Fellow Poet Kyo-won Oh

My fellow poet Oh Kyu-won lives quietly
With one of his lungs on strike,
But my lungs are fine, and I live loudly,
Exploiting my mouth, stomach, and ass.
I drink even when I'm not lonely,
Never worrying about my innards..
They revolt every time
And then resume working again.
I advise him in vain to take good care of his remaining lung
And notice his glasses suddenly glitter...

Dearest Kyu-won,
You will live as long as you have sensation in your gut.

A Brief, Secular Mass for Hwang Inchol, Who Died Too Young

for Hwang Inchol (1940-1993), a lawyer and fellow traveler

1. The Phone Call Telling Me of Your Death

The phone call telling me you're dead oozes from my ear.
My spring orchid wilts.

On the wall, paper-dry mist flowers
surround a pale, dried purple rose
Hanging in air.
Its head and arms stretch down,
Its waist cinched, as if nothing mattered.

Cold water in a cup dries up.
Time, yes, time evaporates.

2. In the Proud Sky

Today in the proud sky
There are many clouds

Among those many clouds
You're the one that emptied yourself out,
Bringing life-giving rain to this world.

The few bare trees
On the winter cliff
Stand with their claws firmly buried under ground.
Over the few hills beyond the empty field,
Above the dim horizon
A cloud suddenly loses its shape.

A Skeleton That Smiles Properly

To make my skeleton smile properly
I've wandered life's loose road in rain and snow,
Even banging my head on the ground now and then
For fifty five summers and winters.

Sometimes, at a construction site
I become a torn sieve
While sifting coarse words.
My entire mind's in shreds.

Beating a skeleton with a stone
Makes the sound of a stone.
Beating it with wood
Makes the sound of wood.

All to make my skeleton smile properly.

S.O.S.

1

Quietly opening the door of a matchbox-size apartment
One match leaves.
Pushing the elevator button
One match leaves.
Shh!
One match leaves
For the place where trees quietly watch human beings.
A tree bends to stretch its waist
A thin match leaves
Timidly.
The phosphor on its head won't flare up easily.

2

The Han River hasn't frozen for the past few years.
Even in winter, the houses in this village are damp.
Ah, winter must have vanished for good.
Waiting for spring when there is no winter!
I'd like to go back to the old village where I knew winter.
Where spring came secretly to the river at dawn
And broke the ice on the river so near my bed.
I want to go inside the sharp sound of cracking ice.
Let me go inside the sound.
Let me go at dawn
To the time when ice still lived.
Ah, once again
The crack of ice!

Flowers in Cement Country

Suffering from the flu
I've skipped breakfast.
I pause my car at the apartments' entrance,
And beckon other cars to go first.
Today I take an alley that goes past a roundabout.
Above, cement walls are stained with yesterday's rain.
I see unfamiliar faces:
This house has rare apple flowers.
That house has hawthorns freshly moved from the mountains,
The house next door has white peonies with fresh green leaves,
And the next house has a cage for a yellow bird,
But it's empty today. Ah, the door's ajar!
Even nature would adore
The naked sunshine above the cement.
A car behind me honks.
I flash my emergency lights:
"Patience, if you please.
I'm nursing now
At nature's breast."

In Last Night's Dream

Last night I dreamed the groaning earth.
After the acid rain ceased,
The streets looked clean,
But the warm apricot flowers hadn't fully bloomed,
And every river looked like the dark sewer beneath Chonggye-chon.
Cars, once called "new Western ghosts" sped past,
And I was breathless, though no-one was chasing me.
In one corner of my dream
A crooked eight-leaved plant on the veranda
Was about to open
(Yes, was about to open) its clubbed hand.

A Dandelion in My Apartment

Last winter, I grew plants on my veranda
With the living room door open,
I left them out.
On a cold day I opened the veranda door wide.
On a colder day, I woke up shivering in the middle of the night
And drew the drapes aside.

Two orchids died.
Now spring has finally arrived.

A dandelion bloomed and withered.
One morning
In the pot for a ficus tree,
I find a globe of dandelion seeds big as a ping-pong ball.
I blow on it, seeds scatter.
I turn and look around. They've disappeared.
If I, too, have to leave this world,
I'd like to leave without a trace,
On my veranda at spring's peak.

Why is Morundae in Chongson?

—O, Earth, Save the Sky!

1

Poet Kim Myong-In and I planned
To defy the plan,
To escape the map and draw a new one.
Riding in his car, I exclaim,
Let's go to the East Sea!
The poet, having only a light breakfast, drives as if doing gymnastics.
Perhaps worried about the future of Korean poetry,
(The heck with the future!)
Until we reach Chinbu, entrance to the real Kangwon.

2

Impulsively, we take a newly paved road.
Such contrast between Mt. Odae's stream and Pyongchang's hills!
The contrast between hill and sky!
The sky is growing deep blue,
We leave the windows open and bathe in fresh forest air.
Who would dare to build a dam here, to ruin the scene?
Who would dare drown the spirit of the gigantic tree?
Drunk on the fragrance of the trees,
We miss the shortcut to Samchok
And have to drive the deep green valley to Chongson.

3

I no longer believe that any lines, any forms, or any colors will save the human mind. I no longer believe that any belief can save humankind's beliefs. But I believe that this deep green of nature, briefly existing between spring and fall, this color without any line, any shape, any sound, offers the warmest embrace and the stillest time of all. When we stop for French fries, a wave-wing butterfly flies toward us, hesitates. Will it fly toward spring or fall? Stay on that yellow wildflower's petals, I pray, amidst this enchanting pasture of green.

4

For the past few years Chongson has been my secret dream, my unfinished poem, my sweetheart, the sweet air I breathe, and the pure unpaved road of my life. Rough roads petted too much and ruined the muffler of my car, but now all the roads are paved. Tunnels were built beneath the pass, the road to Kangneung was constructed, and the non-stop route from Chinbu opened. Now scattered litter, broken wine bottles, and old signboards saying, "Danger" are the only traces of my dim flame. Today even the mountains that once enchanted my soul crouch vacantly. Still, over the mountains blue sky remains, the spirit of the color blue.

5

At Morundae, the familiar pine we met last time greets us.
The tree looks more natural after a lighting strike.
The only change, more lichen-broken rocks.
Even the weekday afternoon's serenity is the same.
Look, below the cliff, white ducks swim.
What embraces those ducks?
Ah, blue sky.
The ducks swim in the sky.
A clay-like clump of green falls in.
Splash!
The sky becomes deep blue.
The exciting harmony between earth and sky!
I tightly close my eyes.
Suddenly my fellow traveler bursts into laughter
And the lightning-struck tree,
Yes, by secretly slowing time's flow,
Barely saves me from falling down.

Part II
from *Journey to Morundae*
(1991)

Journey to Morundae

1

I choose to remain alone, avoiding people, in crowded Seoul.
I sit alone among younger people drinking draft beer in a bar,
Close the blinds to block memories melting in summer heat.
Suddenly the idea of becoming a lone traveler takes root.
Will there be tourists even in a deserted mine?
This is the season when serene roads vanish from the map.
I lock my office,
Where I spent entire days, even during summer vacation,
Spread the map, and draw a circle in red.
I leave before dawn the the next day.

2

Purposely avoiding Chŏng-ryong port
I drive down highway thirty-one.
I leave the highway at Chillang
And take a local unpaved road.
Beside the road, a stream swells with chrome-yellow water,
Stained from the filtering of ore.
I downshift, and my Hyundai "Presto" runs fast indeed.
I pray to the road god that the car won't fail
As I pass a shoulder where horseweed flowers thrive.
Adagio.
I climb a steep slope where a dump truck's tracks run deep.
The road god eases the sharp curve,
Revealing a precipitous cliff.
The chrome-yellow stream becomes
Dreamlike Negro spirituals and begins to flow.
Tuning in to the melancholy tone of the spirituals,
I pass a huge heap of decaying trash.
I drive my small car slowly, sweating with the air-conditioner off.
Ah! On the cliff is a deserted mine, its black mouth wide open.
Above the lips, a tile roof protrudes
And above that,

Like a beard, unkempt grass.
Two beams of rusty steel protrude from the ground
Like an old man's remaining teeth.
At the entrance, a rusty coal cart stands on the twisted rails
As if coming out of the pit.
Afraid of being eaten by the dark,
I enter timidly, with my head low.
Momentarily deaf.
Ah! The scent of the people who disappeared!
A drop of water falls from the ceiling,
Lands directly on my head.

3
The hill is steep.
I travel the road to Chŏng-am Temple
Where the *sariva* of the Buddhist priest Chajang rest peacefully.
He, too, must have panted while climbing this hill.
I feel like abandoning my wheezing car.
Wait. Why did the great Buddhist priests Chajang and Uisang,
Desert the glorious Kyŏngju, Hwangryongsa, and Pusoksa,
And chose to wander the remote mountains of Kangwon?

Why did Chajang choose to enter Nirvana in the deep mountains of Kangwon?
Didn't Uisang, whose place of Nirvana is unknown,
Also roam the deep valley of Kangwon?
Perhaps somewhere near here?
I climb the steep hill,
Until I reach 4,200 feet.
The well-known Manhang Pass suddenly appears.

This is where Yŏngwol and Chŏngson meet.
I turn the rattling engine off, get out, look down
Waves of pine, fir, and spruce
In silvery waves,
Pure skin of unpaved road between.
Surely fresh, raw, raw virgin land!

Suddenly my mouth waters.
In the deep valley below,
Neither the pagoda of Hwangryong nor skyscrapers can be seen.
I'm cool, though there's no wind.
Momentarily risking my life, I whip my car around on the steep hill
Toward Chŏngson,
Quickly passing Hwangryong Temple, Building 63, and Chŏng-am Temple.

4

At the motel near Hwaam natural spring, the smiling receptionist says,
"No rooms available in all Chŏngson tonight.
It's the peak season of the year, you know.
There's a convention in town, besides.
I'm afraid you'll have to drive through the night to Yŏngwol or Pyŏngch'ang.
But first see the sunset here."
After eating mushroom soup,
I hit the road again.
Such fresh and marvelous cliffs:
Their faces glow in the dusk.
I travel to the end of the road beneath bright clouds.

5

Morundae Mountain was absolutely calm.
I could hear pollen falling on the river.
I sat there, not realizing it was getting dark.
A bird eyed me suspiciously while flying by.
Mosquitoes randomly bit me.
(Love of something fresh and raw!)
Sitting there, completely drenched,
I wasn't lonely at all.

The Koryŏ Burial

Last night, I dreamed I was taken for a Koryŏ burial.
On a sloping path in the sparse pine woods
My son gravely pulled the cart,
My daughter pushed from behind, and my wife wept
As they carried me to the burial site.
The towering cross on a new church pierced
the overcast sky.
Passing a country school, children played soccer at recess.
I implored my family, foolishly, to stop
So I could run with them one last time.
My voice didn't even reach my ears,
Perhaps because of the tangled orange hedge.
Oh, that was close!
A few white violets, their purple veins exposed
Escaped the crushing wheels of the cart.
The soil around them glowed.

Kwanak Diaries 1

After stepping out to see the first snow,
I boil water for my green tea.
As the sky softens, light snowflakes dance,
Like white tea leaves from the southern coast
Scattered all over the sky.
As I gaze at the falling snow
I envision snow-covered nutmeg woods.

The classroom is empty.
It's three in the afternoon.
I check the schedule. Ah, my class began at two.

I return to my office and open the door.
Just before turning on the light
I'm surprised to see a familiar, middle-aged man
Sitting on the sofa in the darkness.

"Don't be alarmed. I'm you.
Look at these new glasses.
See the scratch made when you dropped them in a pub two days ago?
Here's the wallet that holds your social security card, faculty I.D.,
        Credit cards, and driver's license.
Here's the memo book with all the phone numbers you recently changed.
I'll take your four o'clock class. You just rest."

I turn on the light.
Nobody's there.

Who am I?

Kwanak Diaries 2

—for my friend, Lee Sangok

Students wearing red headbands strike a gong,
Shout their demonstration slogans.
Someone slams a door in the hall.
The gong's sound turns my books red.

Teaching
Is like singing an aubade while gazing at the stars.
Although stars shine in seven different colors,
Their light is different from dawn's.

The protesters' drumbeat rings in my ears.
Let's see,
Teaching:
Is it threatening at gunpoint, forcing words into brains?
And then when the space is filled
Close the door and turn the key?
I see day breaking beyond the tracks.

The gong rings in my ears again.
This is timorous hell, but I'm unable to retreat to my books.
I plan to flee to heaven, to a tavern ablaze with infernal flames.
But I turn back, once again.

Forgetting My Army I.D.

A few days ago, being issued a license at the D.A.O.,
The clerk asked for my army I.D..
A sudden flash:
Ah, I can't remember!
Wait, it took me thirty years to forget.
Much has changed in all that time:
Roadside trees, addresses, taverns, people I met and left.
Now I'll let go of all of them,
And go to a place free of licenses and I.D.s,
Where numberless flowers freely bloom and die,
And though they may not be exotic fragrances,
Each has its own scent

A complete stranger, at last.

Sleeping in Pyŏngch'ang

Please, don't drive on highway thirty-one
From Changpyŏng to Pyŏngch'ang on summer evenings.
And please, don't drive alone,
For if you drive, you'll squash and pulverize
The swarms of frogs that lie down
On the warm road that runs along Pyŏngchang River.
The pools of blood!
Look at that frog. With just one leg, he can jump higher than the rest.
My car dashes toward the spot where he lands.

It's twenty miles from Changpyŏng to Pyŏngch'ang
A rookie executioner, I drive like mad,
Listening attentively to Pyŏngch'ang's night rain,
Drinking whiskey once again.

The Bread of This World

Even after reading all the books I own,
I've found no proof there's a tavern in heaven, a cluttered study, a dream.
Or leaves falling outside the window
And brief twilight drenching mountain peaks.

In heaven, it may be brighter than this world's day.
Our spirits may applaud and celebrate,
We may dine on gourmet restaurants' buffets,
We'll may no longer need medical insurance,
Or any retirement plan.

Outside my study
The familiar magpie sitting in a half-bare maple tree
Joyfully nods to me,
And I immerse myself in a sea of dreams,
A gift only living creatures receive.

If Mankind Wants to Survive

If mankind wants to survive
And continue to walk the earth,
All countries should live like a stylish young man.

Like a young man, like a young man

Who tries in vain to grow orchids and ponders suicide,
Who shoots firecrackers instead of cannonballs,
and knows what discipline is,
Who wanders, enchanted, to the harbor on his way back home one day
And stows away in the bosom of a foreign ship.

Like a young man, like a young man.

Stingray

Among the fish on the counter
At the market,
(How decent they are, compared to mammals!)
The stingray seems the saddest.
Oh, stingray!
Lying there so languidly,
Even your eyes seem closed.
But you, bird of the sea,
Fly gracefully amidst the waves.
Ah! Look at your dynamic shape
As you finish your flamenco
And rest.

Plum Blossom

After the mountain rain stopped,
The scent of plum blossoms revived
I inhaled deeply.
My head cleared,
And my vision brightened,
Like a light that flashes briefly,
And remains visible long after it's disappeared.

Listening to "A Survivor from Warsaw" by Schoenberg

Those not destroyed in the face of death are beautiful.
Even in movies about war,
There's beauty in refusing to collapse, choosing death.
Almost collapsing, still flowing, it never overflows,
This elaborate twelve-tone piece!
When we walk inside music
We become bright lights.

My Heart Aches Today

None of the village's big trees
Are free from wounds.
"Is there an unwounded soul in the world?"*
Today my heart's aches,
And though I try to hide the wound,
Through the whole afternoon and evening,
Thick fluid flows from me.
Still it can't be healed
And throbs with pain.
Wait, I'd rather discuss my pain
With my fellow poet, Rimbaud,
Who's the same age as my son.
Let's talk for a while.
Is there an unwounded soul in this world?

*A line from a poem by Rimbaud.

The Road to T'omal

When time, like ideology, presses me
And the phone rings ceaselessly, even at night,
To the place all dreamers dream of
I must go.

To the end of the road and the end of the dream,
To a place like T'omal in Haenam,
Where I can climb to the observatory
On a winter day before camellias bloom.
To see the island-dusted South Sea, transcending time and space,
Harmonize with seagulls, so pretty flying in a flock,
I must go.

To a place where nutmeg trees
Shout loudly,
Press their lips to the wind.

Part III:
Wind Burial Poems & Love Songs
(1991-1993

Wind Burial 17

A drop of water
Falls to the ground.
How spectacular it would be
If my camera caught that moment!
(If only my mind could stop time!)
It splashes instantly,
Creating a crown
Or spreads like thin fog across the garden
Inducing, in the flowers, thirst.

When the water comes toward earth,
Every drop is thrilling.
It falls like a ripe apple
Bouncing in ecstasy.
Rolling slowly over,
It lies down peacefully.

Wind Burial 18

What is an awakening?

It may be grasping the earth's hand and not letting go,
The hand that pulls my arms, legs, and body toward the center of the earth
On a weary day.
(Ah, a tight fit.)
It may be the floating steam of my breath.
It may be the rainbow painted by the rubbing raindrops.

It may be a flower-like wind that doesn't die
Whenever I turn to see it.

Wind Burial 19

Oh, how I wish to render into words
The blazing colors of autumn leaves
Glowing above scattered white reeds
In this late autumn!

Perhaps I should pull out a series of thoughts
Like a rope full of knots
And put them on the autumn leaves
Just to burn them!

Wind Burial 20

The sea's wet,
Like a wild rose,
a drenched crown jewel
Like colored lips
Which part to reveal a world of color.
Her lips are wet.
When her lips part, there's a dazzling sea
And radiant white sand.

Soaked to the bone,
The sea crawls back onto earth.

Wind Burial 21

That instinct!
Not only in man, but in every living thing.
Even micro-organisms,
That instinct constantly breathes.
Even lifeless new materials,
When sharply bent,
Instinctively try to return to their original peaceful form.

Trees, flowers, grass swaying in the wind,
The bobbing Adam's apple of a squirrel eating nuts;
Those things can't be captured
Even in photographs in biology books..

Wind Burial 22

It floats,
The boat without an oar.
Today it's still.
Enduring the itch to leave.

It doesn't know
If it floats on sea, sky,
Or heat.

Like a witless monkey
Leaving his tree the first time
Doesn't know whether
He'll float on the ground.

Or reluctant as a human being to wear out
And return to the starting point,
It doesn't know whether
It floats on the core of life.

Wind Burial 23

When the body becomes old,
Even athletic feet leave for a younger one.
When the athlete's feet have left,
Will the old feet be haunted
Or blessed?

Father says:
"Cremation is like dying twice,
So bury me in a sunny place when I'm dead."

I replied: "Of course," but a question began to arise:
What difference does it make if we die twice?
Three times? Even four?
If we endure cremation's flames
We might find Hell's fire nice,
Those huge charcoal flames.

Smoke timidly rises above the hill.

Wind Burial 24

When peonies bloom on the veranda
I write a letter to a far-away friend,
To tell him another friend has just died.
I write about the peonies instead.

As I wash my face and hair tonight,
The moon has set and the earth begins to rise.

Wind Burial 25

I approached Bong-am temple at Mt. Hui-yang

Late autumn evening
Ankle-deep in autumn leaves,
The sound of the creek seeps in,
The sound of wind plunges into leaves.
Late autumn evening.

When I stop in my tracks,
The sounds of nature stop.
All traces of moving things cease.
When I look up,
I see the summit of Mt. Hui-yang
Quietly burning white. Burning bright.

The air is colored violet-jade
And returns to the sky where it belongs.
After ceasing its diffusion,
After escaping the spectrum
And disappearing into the universe
Light slants, becomes translucent.
Oh, such marvelous hues!

Just in time,
The mountaintop
Burns white.

Wind Burial 26

Why didn't the Bodhidharma become emaciated
During the nine years he spent in meditation?
Why did his legs degenerate,
Rather than his body grow thin?
Why did he endure silently,
In pain and ecstasy,
(The silent moans, the screams,
The laugh of organs, the suicidal explosion.)
Why did he endure so long,
Smiling at his body's every waiting cell?

What is waiting? What is degeneration?
Perhaps evolution is nothing but running from degeneration?
Perhaps evolution just refers to the limbs and body of a man
Who constantly misses his step and staggers backward
Until he stands against a wall?

Wind Burial 27

When I leave this world
I'll take my two hands, two feet, and my mouth.
I'll take my dim eyes, too, carefully covering them with my lids.
But I'd rather leave my ears,
Ears keen to catch the sound of late night rain
As it gives its arm to autumn's shoulder.
Ears that know which autumn tree stands in rain
Only by listening
Will be left.

Wind Burial 28

When I finally depart this world
I'll take along
The air which fills my lungs,
Even if I have to throw everything else away,
Even if I have to thwart the moisture on my tongue.
My chest may feel tight,
But I'll take along my last breath
When I briefly rest to rub my tired feet along the way,
And look back on the world I've just departed,
I'll see people swarming and giggling in every city,
To laugh just once more
I'll carry the air in my lungs with me.
To laugh heartily one last time.

Wind Burial 29

On both sides of Nirvana Pavilion valley on Mt. Odae
I hear the sound of a hidden water flow.
It spreads far today due to misty rain,
Serene as empty space in a writer's amateur painting,
And my heart's at peace.
Today, even trout lilies didn't raise their heads.
Only wild camellias bloomed,
Frequently stopped my steps.
Descending from the empty Sangwon temple.
I drank from a murmuring stream
As if it were a natural spring.
Oh, may the sound of flowing water remain in my body
May it flow through my body, deep underground,
Whether I'm awake or asleep.

Wind Burial 30

On a peony branch,
In the middle of copulation
A female praying mantis begins to devour her mate,
Beginning with his head.
A pleasant sensation as the head vanishes from earth!
Not a single blade of dry grass to lean on,
With its entire body exposed,
It rubs against the entire universe.
A cosmic convulsion!

Wind Burial 31

Rubbing dried chrysanthemums
Releases a sweet fragrance.
How light the scent!
Gazing at the palm of my hand,
My heart gushes out.

Lightly as a butterfly or a dayfly
With the heart of a plant sown in,
I'll drift about
Wearing the flower's lingering scent.

Wind Burial 32

On an autumn day
Softly rubbing against a blade of grass,
Changing the body fragrance a bit
With a crisp sound,
After bidding farewell secretly to stalks and roots of grass
With twin-clock eyes and red tails,
Into that space of red-tailed dragonflies,
I'll enter as a boy, an insect net raised high.

Wind Burial 33

My wife tells me there's an odor coming from my body
At last I'm beginning to decompose!
First my mouth rots
And then my asshole decays.

The tranquil early winter sunlight coming in that window.
Is drying my mind clean.

One spring day,
When my mouth and asshole are dust,
I wonder if the wine in my fellow poet's house
The wine that enchants my body from head to toe
Will continue to ferment?

Wind Burial 34

I'll rise and go, go to the outer limits of the universe
Where naked snowflakes do a livelier dance
Than they do in the sky.
I'll rise and go, go to the outer edge of Seoul
Where huge snowflakes take off their pollution-stained clothes,
even their undergarments,
Dancing and flying naked
Until they become the dance.

Where snowflakes wear only six-crystal feathers.

Wind Burial 35

At the funeral home,
I bow twice in front of the picture of my dead friend.
The image laughs as if saying:
Nothing has really changed
except my body's atoms, a tiny bit.
The sound of rain outside,
The sound of mourners playing cards and drinking in the next room,
Even the sound of slippers scuffing toward the bathroom remains the same.

Wind Burial 36

My final joy is diving
Stepping on the verse's accelerator again and again
Until my field of vision narrows
And my eyes open to a bunch of bright autumn leaves
Over a precipice on Mt. Sorak, my seatbelt fastened,
Diving.

Between my body and empty sky
Lies only zero millimeters of space.
Ah, the autumn leaves
Blazing inside my eyes!

Wind Burial 37

Does it matters if I become a rueful spirit and wander endlessly,
Unable to bury my feet beneath the earth,
Among all kinds of other rueful spirits,
A feather-light spirit,
Unable to utter a doleful cry,
or just malingering in sleep,
Imply weeping for a moment at dusk,
Just before it abruptly disappears.

Wind Burial 38

In the morning, when it's time for coffee
My mouth tells my stomach,
'I'm sending a cup of coffee now."
In a moment, the stomach will speak to the bowels,
"A liquid that's a little irritating to you has just passed through."
Around evening, the bowels will send a message to the mouth.
"The host can't sleep."

Wind Burial 39

Traveling in groups,
Sleepless nights
In motels at the far end of ports,
No matter how drunk I was,
I could lie down
Only after I determined who else was snoring there.
Those sleepless nights!
At the end of sleeplessness, alone, I opened the window
And spied with the streetlight on dancing snowflakes
Right before they threw their bodies into the waves of the sea!

But these days, even among bags and bundles,
I lie down and fall asleep as easily
As a red dragonfly dozing off on dry leaves of grass.
While someone next to me toys with literature and life,
I fall asleep with my ears open,
Trusting my innards, one by one, to the last drops of wine.

Wind Burial 40

Greeting the plum blossoms at Sonam Temple,
Breathing their scent into my chest,
Feeling their scent on my skin,
Absorbing their scent inside,
I tumbled like a soft bee drunk on honey,
And met the buzzing bees.

Suddenly the bees flying in the air,
Started to laugh wholeheartedly,
Each one turned over
And, like a plum blossom, bloomed.

Am I outside the plum blossoms?
Or is the temple inside of them?

Wind Burial 41

What a wonder the blue peacock flower is!
As I go into the petal that looks like a yellow or blue butterfly,
Passing through the mouth and even through the throat of a butterfly,
Like stealthily going through a revolving door,
I see the honey bubbles.
The bubbles become bigger and bigger
Until they finally explode.
The spring so sweet.

Wind Burial 42

I poured my heart into the Bibichu flower
Blooming at Baekryon Temple in Muju.

The ten purple flowers hanging on each stalk
Glow like Buddhist lanterns just blown out.
Bibichu sways gently in the wind,
Each flower lantern shaped like
A white crescent moon.

Oh, Bibichu, drink me,
I can't drink you.
I can only hasten to you, blooming on the roadside,
And explode toward you.

Drink me, Bibichu.
Drink me, who explodes like water from winter's burst pipe.

Finally,
I'll return as a pipe
That can no longer contain itself.

Wind Burial 43

Ah! I've listened to all the music.
I've listened too much to Beethoven's string quartets,
I've plunged into the melody of the *Kayakeum*,
And my stone valley orchid died of neglect.
Yesterday I fell asleep, listening to Brahm's clarinet quintet.
Now I wish to forget all of East and West
And live in a room filled with wind orchids,
Without stereo, phone, or telegram.

The sound of wind leaving after prolonged play.

Wind Burial 44

The whispering sounds of the wind,
The mountain awkwardly sitting behind the village,
Feel familiar, like in my hometown.
The stepping stones barely crossing the stream,
Seem familiar, as if they were my own.
If I squint, everything looks familiar:
Even the tree's shy gestures as it sways to the voice of the wind.
One clear day,
If I close my eyes completely,
Won't everything look astonishingly familiar?

Ah, the delightful sounds of human beings!

Wind Burial 45

For a few days, for some reason, I felt ill.
The bookcase doors were all open wide
The books were lined up, as if leaving on a trip,
Some wore thick winter coats.

Outside, autumn sunlight blurs my vision.
Store signs are crystal clear.
People passing by are transparent.
Even the long slender arms of a girl carrying books are clear,
Dangerously close to a street full of dashing cars
Even the road's smooth shoulders are clear.
Even time's soft caress of its shoulder is clear.
My eyes are open.
Oh, my eyes.

Carry this corpse away!

Wind Burial 46

Living on the northern slope of Mt. Kwanak,
I've often seen the mountain hidden in fog,
Sometimes drizzling rain clears the fog,
And the fog embraces the rain.
When I have to leave the things I cherish in my heart,

When I have to return them before I go,
I'll return Mt. Kwanak first,
The hermit's hut I used to visit,
And finally the water gourd belonging to the hut.
I'll return the rain that lightly falls on the earth,
The rain that skillfully gropes about the ground and stops
Just before darkness falls on a late autumn night.

Wind Burial 47

1992. Evening. Late fall.
This time of the year, no one watches the setting sun.
Below the veranda of an apartment building in Sadang-dong is a parking lot
Where no one listens to the whisper of the wind.

A ficus tree on my veranda.
While the other trees wither away, it endures.
I embrace it with my half-naked body
To reaffirm its body heat.
In an apartment parking lot in Sadang-dong.
No one listens to the whisper of the wind.

On the veranda a slightly bent human figure stands
Like a stroke from a calligraphy brush.

Wind Burial 48

As the wind's touch cools,
And day turns to dusk,
I desire to fall asleep alone,
Wrapped softly in dry blades of grass.
Lifeblood, don't fall asleep.
Do not fall asleep.
Above Mt. Chilgap, less than two-thousand feet high,
Which you can climb by car,
There, the sky is full of stars,
Full of stars.
Where sky and my heart intersect,
Stars twinkle
Like clusters of fixed sparks,
Spread to the horizon and beyond.
Lifeblood, don't fall asleep.

Wind Burial 49

One late autumn evening, alone, I encounter the Aurage River,
A good place to drag my body into and let go.
In the midst of the mountain
Half-bare trees bathe in the sun's last rays.
Around them pine trees calmly stand,
Gazing at two streams that flow down and unknowingly merge.
Two streams awkwardly converge, producing one calm river.
An empty boat floats there, rocking endlessly.
Time does not form a mass.

If I grow too weary of dragging my body
I'll leave it on a ridge
Just like a flowing stream
Looking in vain for its twin.

Wind Burial 50

Today I threw away all my maps.
Wandering the seashore
I wish to stand in glaring snow.
I wish to see an island across the sea
Turn silvery in silence
And then gradually fade in the midst of falling snow.
Then I wish to return from that disappearing island,
And pluck out the islands of my heart.
Pluck out those cherished lands
And the time trapped in my heart.

Today I threw away all my maps.

Wind Burial 51

I leave the narrow-track that runs between Suwon and Inchon,
And walk.
Suddenly the sound of wild geese stops.
One barren mountain hides behind another,
Not fading away, but thinning on top.
The railroad passes the village by.
Nothing happens here.
Chickens scratch the winter ground.
A wristwatch appears between a chicken's toes.
I pull it out. Still ticking.

Could this mean time hidden behind another time?

Wind Burial 52

One late winter evening when fine snow falls,
With neither flowers nor illness left
I'll meet again
My long-forgotten innocence orchids.
I'll meet again
Times I've only now I begun to seek,
(Where are my glasses?)
Though they've been by my side all along.
I'll shake hands and trade places with a pillar
At Pusok Temple's Hall of Eternal Life
Where the exquisite lines of the slightly raised eaves
Extinguish the glow of all other magnificent lines.
I'll stand there in the fine snow
Supporting those graceful lines with my two arms.

And I won't worry when, someday, I crack.

A Poor Love Song 1

Like a small river that smells the sea,
I flow,
Past homes in the last village
And a small stone bridge.
A few nets are loosely strung about.

Beyond the field the dark sky lies,
Deep blue.

A Poor Love Song 2

Summer,
Our summer has ended.
Everything we knew has cooled.
Longing to see the sun's ripe face,
I drove all night long
And arrived at the East Sea by dawn.
There I glimpsed the sun
That traveled behind clouds all morning,
Revealing himself to no one as he softly moved on.

A Poor Love Song 3

Yesterday, the evening rain I longed for didn't come,
And I became a vast desert,
Not immense as the Sahara or the Gobi,
But of a tiny size not normally found in a book,
A desert with only a few mirages.
Traces of wind were drawn on sand;
A bird shadow passed a while ago.
Otherwise, there was nothing.
Wait! There are traces of travelers.
No matter how hard the wind blows, they won't erase.
I follow those footprints and return to where I started,
Not finding an oasis where water gushes forth, trees grow.

A Poor Love Song 4

Just before spring begins to bud
While observing the violently blossoming snowbell tree,
Without knowing, we turn to each other
And gaze into each other's eyes.
For a moment
The retina opens and closes, clicking,
Capturing the sky.

What a moment!

A Poor Love Song 5

Between two hills, looking to everyone
Like an unfinished painting,
A half-drawn rainbow hangs.
Yet it's still a rainbow: there is no hidden part.

Nothing is inside my heart, except my heart.

Unknowingly
My heart
Flows toward the ground.

A Poor Love Song 6

Despite the light autumn rain,
There are no rainbows,
Only thickening evening fog.
Even in daylight
I could pass unnoticed.
My heart slowly cools.
I read the evening paper on the subway,
Then left it on the seat when I got off.
I returned to my apartment by bus.
The flowers in the shop smiled dishearteningly.
Nothing happened.

((Help!))

A Poorer Love Song 1

At the foot of a hill spring has abandoned,
Amid colorful flowers,
Stands my childhood friend's house.
His youngest daughter brings me strawberries on a salver.
Her waist and face radiant, her hand a clubhand.

Beneath that imperturbable face
A hydrangea blooms,
Undulating cool, deep shade.

A Poorer Love Song 2

Today foggy rain fell
Then rose back to the sky.
Didn't it want to wet the dusty earth?
While walking the streets, invisible in a crowd,
I'm at peace.
I look around and peep into shops.
Soon even foggy rain will avoid me.
I'll continue to wander in a crowd,
Looking for rain to wet my body.

A Poorer Love Song 3

To keep you from appearing in my songs
I've traveled far and wide.
I've been to the East Sea, the South Sea
Even to Tomal in Haenam.
Once, while dodging a truck
My car crashed in a rice field.
My glasses flew off, landing on the floor.
My seat-belted shoulder hurt.
There was really nothing more.
I stood with the others, watching
My wounded car, its engine killed.

A Poorer Love Song 4

I visit the South Sea every year
But I've never seen camellias in full bloom.
In 1991, I went to Tongyoung in late February just to see them.
All the camellias drooped, frozen, on the sides of the road
Due to sudden cold.
Was it only camellias that drooped?
No, I was drooping, too,
Freezing in my heater-broken car.

A Poorer Love Song 5

In late winter, traveling alone around Koje Island,
I completed one cycle of my life.
Wherever I went, fishing ports hid their inner view.
The sea, like a lake trapped between island and open sky,
Hid a windbreak forest and a labyrinthine shipyard.
I had a drink with construction workers:
The side dish of sushi was superb.
While re-crossing Koje Bridge, I heard
The chiseling sound of an iron pen
Carving the sea on the globe,
The sea that repeatedly hides and appears.

A Poorer Love Song 6

Spring came reeling in.
I took the plants out to my veranda.
My neighbor's plants were already out.
An early honeybee,
Flying not to the sky nor the earth,
But to my apartment on the eighth floor,
Between the earth and the sky,
Flew off without looking back.
The plants shivered,
Their feet buried in those cold pots.
Did they miss their embryonic stage
When their body and soul were one in a seed?
As I shook my head I knew
Something had dried up in my heart.

The Poorest Love Song 1

Once I dove into frozen rivers
To collect the grim faces of heavy rocks.
These days I roam quietly
To collect light feathers left by birds.
I've gathered the familiar magpie's breast feathers
And yellow wing feathers of some nameless bird.
(Did I want to fly?)
I found the feathers of a sparrow or a swallow eaten by a hawk.
The silence of those bloody feathers
So deep it can't be broken
Even in the language of birds.

The Poorest Love Song 2

Taoists live with their eyes half closed
Perhaps to hide empty minds.
The silence of an empty mind,
Even pots brought in from the veranda's cold are hushed.
A butterfly,
Reluctant to fly in such silence,
Reluctant to become an idea,
Flew away as a butterfly.

The Poorest Love Song 3

After ten years of waiting
I set out on at last at dawn on my trip
To see the plum flowers at Sonam Temple.
To clear my mundane thoughts
I deliberately dropped by Tamyang
And looked leisurely around the Museum of Bamboo Crafts,
The stone flagpole and the five-story stone pagoda.
Then I slowly approached the ticket booth at the temple entrance.
Walking toward the temple, I constantly inhaled
But smelled only faint vestiges of plum flowers in quietude.
Nine out of ten buds had frozen in the recent cold,
Only a few petals hung on each stem.
(Shouldn't ten years be long enough to wait?)
I saw no butterflies, no birds, no spring, and no ten years.

The Poorest Love Song 4

These days *Lady Spring Fragrance* seem as trivial
As *Romeo and Juliet.*
Lee Mongryong drives a cab in South Seoul
And Spring Fragrance grows old in Chongno.
Romeo opens a fencing school in suburban Rome
And Juliet a shop near the Spanish Steps in Rome's heart.
Though a bit expensive, I stop there and buy a tie.
No-one wants to read a novel or a play these days.
Rather than becoming a tormented literature lover
Perhaps it would be better to just live like this.

But would it really be?
As I leave the shop, the tie in a paper bag,
I suddenly spin around,
My finger protruding from my jacket.
Pretending to have a gun, I imagine that I shout:
"Hands up!"

The Poorest Love Song 5

I'm locked in a universe
Where I can't surpass the speed of light,
Though I spring out at lightning speed
And travel at light's velocity,
I can't escape, no matter how hard I try.
My body flies along behind.
(Look back!
Without my flesh and bones,
I look like a roof tangled with clay and fresh grass.)
But you're always one corner ahead.
Everything is so dark.
Walking aimlessly I arrive at a strange city's terminal.
Everything is so dark
Except two streetlights in the public square
And the station's lighted clock.
It's midnight.
Ah, it's not yet time!

The Poorest Love Song 6

Since you went to a place so far away,
Farther than the expressway can reach
More remote than Cheju or Sorok,
Since the sky collapsed behind you,
Everything has become so light.
Even leashed dogs being dragged along
And chunks of concrete embedded all over the city.

(Nothing but the mind exists in my mind.)

Nothing but autumn exists in autumn flowers.
Nothing but sky exists in sky.
Nothing but height exists in acrophobia.
Looking down from the top of a fifteen-story building,
Straggling Chinese asters embroider the parking lot.

Nothing but time exists in time (oh my!).

Notes on the Poems

Mishi Pass (Mishinyong) A mountain pass located at the edge of Soraksan National Park in the north eastern province of Kangwon-do.

P'ohang: This is the largest city on Korea's east coast. Headquarters of the second-largest steel mill in the world, the city is on the East Sea (The Sea of Japan).

Wonhyo: A prominent seventh-century Buddhist priest during the Shilla Dynasty. At a time when most Buddhist monks tended to study in T'ang Dynasty China, Wonhyo decided to remain in Korea to become an original and creative Buddhist. Later developed Mahayana Buddhism and heavily influenced Japanese Buddhism.

Soju: A popular Korean liquor.

Ho Nansolhon: A famous Korean woman writer who lived in the Chosun Dynasty. Her brother, Ho Kyun, was the celebrated author of the novel *The Story of Hong Kildong.*

Chodang-dong: A district in the city of Kangnung, it is where Ho Nansolhon was born.

Kangnung: The second-largest city on Korea's northeast coast.

Kim Hyon: Pen name of prominent literary critic, Kim Kwangnam. One of the poet's best friends, he died unexpectedly at the age of forty-seven.

So (West) Pyon Jye: One of the two major types of p'ansori. The other is Tong (East) Pyon Jye. So Pyon Jye is said to be feminine whereas Tong Pyon Jye is masculine. Pansori, a story-in-song, was invented in the eighteenth century. The word, p'ansori, is composed of two words *pan* (stage) and *sori* (melody). It is also the title of an award-winning Korean film directed by Im Kwon-Taek.

111

Kwangnam: Real name of the poet's deceased friend, Kim Hyon.

Suyuri: A district in northeastern Seoul.:

Sadang-dong: The Seoul district where the poet has lived since 1990.

Daekwan Pass: A pass located in the Taeback Mountains.:

Bopju temple: A temple on Songni Mountain in Chungbak Province.

Mt Songni: A mountain in Korea's north-central Chungbuk Province.

Yun Sondo: a renowned Sijo poet during the mid-Chosun Dynasty who spent twenty years of his life writing poems as an exile and hermit. His pen name was Kosan.

Kayakeum: A twelve-stringed Korean harp.

Li Po (701-762, A.D.): one of the greatest poets of the T'ang Dynasty. Also known as Li Tai-Po, he was a well-known lover and connoisseur of wine, which always inspired his muse and poetic imagination.

Jin: A Korean liquor.

Mt. Saja: A mountain in Korea's northeastern province of Kangwon .

Mt. OIdae: Another mountain in Kangwon Province.:

Yangpyung: A city in the northern province of Kyongki..

Namhae: The South Sea

Samch'unp'o: A city in Kyongsangnam province on Korea's southeast.

Hongch'on - A town in Kangwon Province.

Kangwon - Province in northeastern Korea, it borders North Korea.

Sambong: A famous spring in Kangwon Province.

Hongch'on: A hot springs resort in Kangwon province.

Chukjang: A mountainous district in Kyonbuk Province.

Bopheung Temple: A temple on Saja Mountain.:

Mt. Saja; Mt. Odae:: Mountains in Kangwon Province.

Ch'ang Wukjin: (1917–1990) A famous Korean painter who embodied Oriental philosophy in his paintings.:

Kimpo: A county in Kyonggi Province in northwestern Korea.

Kanghwa: An island in Kyonggi Province.

Mt. Mani: A mountain on Kangwhwa Island.

Chonggye-chon: Originally a stream, but now a sewer currently running beneath the street called Chonggye-chun in Seoul. The stream was covered with asphalt years ago to build a new

Morundae: A place in Mt. Sorak, which is so spectacular that even the clouds, stopping to watch the enchanting scenery, are said to be enraptured at the scene. The name, "Morundae," means, "Where even the clouds are enthralled by an awesome scenic view."

Chongson: A county in Kwangwon Province.

Chinbu: A small city in Kangwon Province.

Pyongchang; Samchoki: Counties in Kangwon Province

Port Chong-ryong at Yongwol: A famous historic site where the young king T'anjong, who was abdicated by his uncle who then became King Sejo, lived a year in exile in the 15th century until he was killed by the usurper.

Chajang Yulsa: A famous Buddhist monk who built the Punhwangsa Pagoda.

Uisang: A Buddhist monk during the Silla Dynasty who built Pusok Temple and founded Hwaom Chong, a Buddhist sect based on the Avatamska Sutra.

Kyongju: This city of 300,000 in the eastern province of Kyongsangbuk was the capital city of the Silla Dynasty for almost1,000 years.

Hwangryong (Yellow Dragon) Temple: A Buddhist temple built during the Silla Dynasty in the 7th Century (645 A.D.). It was burned and almost destroyed during the Mongolian invasion in 1238, A.D. Originally nine stories high, only three exist today.

Pusok Temple: A temple built by Uisang in 676 A.D. in Pusok county at Youngju, Kyungpuk. Burnt to the ground by early 14th century invaders, it was rebuilt in 1358. It escaped destruction during the Japanese invasions in the 16th century and survives today as the oldest wooden structure in Korea.

Manhang Pass: A mountain pass between Chongson and Yongwol counties in Kangwon Province.

Building 63: A 63-story building in Youido, Seoul. Highest in Korea, it is a representative modernist building owned by Kyobo Life Insurance Company.

Chongson; Yongwol:; Pyongch'ang Counties in Kangwon Province.

Koryo Burial: Ancient burial custom briefly practiced during the Koryo Dynasty (918-1392 A.D.) whereby a dying old person is left to die in an open tomb.

Kwanak: A rugged mountain just southeast of the campus of Seoul National University. Within walking distance of the campus, it is a popular hiking spot

Arnold Schoenberg: (1874-1951) Austrian composer who established serial technique as an important organizational device in music, he was a mentor to Alban Berg.

T'omal: The southernmost point in Korea, it means "land's end."

Haenam: A county in Chonnam Province.:

Wind Burial: A unique burial custom practiced in the southern and western parts of Korea. It was designed to provide a fisherman who sailed out to sea to fish with a chance to see, upon returning, the remains of his deceased parent before burial. Normally, the body is taken to a nearest uninhabited island for a wind burial, and later buried with a ceremony when it had dried up enough.

Bong-am Temple: A temple in Kyongbuk Province.

Mt. Hui-yang: A mountain in Kyongbuk Province.

Bodhidharma: The semi-legendary founder of Zen in China, who is said to have spent nine years in a cave in meditation.

Nirvana Sanctum: Nirvana Sanctum is a memorial chapel for deceased priests in Buddhist temples.

Sangwon temple: A temple on Mt. Odae, which is famous for its ancient bronze bell made in the 8th century.

Spring water: In the deep valleys or mountains of Korea there are some small natural wells made from water falling from the peak of the mountain.

Most Koreans enjoy drinking this crystal-clear mountain water which is called, "medicinal water."

Aurage: Name of a river in Korea. "Aurage" means "merge" in Korean.

Lady Spring Fragrance: A story-in-song (Pansori), the pinnacle of the Korean love story written in the eighteenth century, *Lady Spring Fragrance* is one of the best known vernacular Korean romances. The author, however, is unknown.

Chongno: A major street of commerce and shopping in Seoul, like Bond or Regent Street in London.

Lee Mongryong: The male protagonist of *Lady Spring Fragrance.*

Spring Fragrance: The female protagonist of *Lady Spring Fragrance*

Bibichu: *Hosta Longpipes*. This is an orchid that blooms in July and August in southern Korea.

Mt. Chilgap: A mountain in Chungnam Province.

Koje Bridge: A bridge separating Koje Island and the mainland.

Sonam temple: This temple of the Chogye sect is located in Chogyesan Provncial Park in Sunch'on in the province of Chollanamin Korea's south-west corner.

Cheju: An island fifty-three miles off the southernmost tip of Korea.

Sorok Island: A beautiful island in the South Sea, it is the site of a leper colony.

About the Poet

Tong-Gyu Hwang, born in 1938 in Seoul, Korea, holds a degree in English from Seoul National University and studied at the University of Edinburgh. He participated in the International Writing Program at the University of Iowa, and conducted research at New York University and UC/Berkeley as a Visiting Scholar. Currently, he is Professor of English at Seoul National University.

Hwang, who made his literary debut as a poet in 1958, is the author of eleven collections of poetry including *One Fine Day* (1961), *Wind Burial* (1984), *Who's Afraid of Alligators?* (1986), and most recently *Love Songs, Berkeley Style* (2000). The Wind Burial sequence, which began in 1982, is still growing and expanding. His collection of poems, *Wind Burial* was translated by Grace Loving Gibson and published by St. Andrews Press in 1990. In 1988, *Collected Poems of Hwang Tonggyu*, Volumes I and II were published to commemorate his sixtieth birthday and to celebrate his lifetime achievements.

An internationally acclaimed poet, Hwang won the Modern Literature Award (1968), the Korean Literature Award (1980), the Yonam Literary Award (1988), the Kim Jongsam Literary Award (1991), the Isan Literary Award (1991), and the Daesan Literary Award (1995). His poems have been translated into English, German, French and a host of other languages.

About the Translators

Seong-Kon Kim, born in 1949, studied at Columbia University and the State University of New York at Buffalo, from which he received his Ph.D. in 1984. Author of ten books including *Writers in the Postmodern Age* (1990), *Literature in the Age of New Media* (1996) and *Literature and Film* (1997), he has also translated fifteen books. He has taught at Columbia University, Pennsylvania State University, and Brigham Young University. Currently, Kim is Professor of English and Director of the American Studies Institute at Seoul National University. Kim is editor of the literary quarterly *21st Century Literature* and a regular columnist for the *Dong-A Daily* newspaper.

Dennis Maloney, born in 1951, is a poet, translator, and landscape architect. His published translations from Japanese include *Tangled Hair: Love Songs of Yosano Akiko* and *Between the Floating Mist: Poems of Ryokan*, both in collaboration with Hide Oshiro. His translations from Spanish include *The Naked Woman* by Juan Ramon Jimenez, *The Landscape of Soria* by Antonio Machado and a number of books by Pablo Neruda, including *The Stones of Chile*, *Maremoto/Seaquake* (with Maria Giachetti), *Windows That Open Inward: Images of Chile*, and *Isla Negra* (with Clark Zlotchew). He is the founding publisher and editor of White Pine Press. He makes his home near Buffalo, New York.